FU

Conservatives

A journal for Liberals
to destroy, rant and vent
without getting arrested

By Alex A. Lluch

WS Publishing Group
San Diego, California 92119

FU Conservatives:
A journal for Liberals to destroy,
rant and vent without getting arrested

By Alex A. Lluch
Published by WS Publishing Group
San Diego, California 92119
© Copyright 2010 by WS Publishing Group

Design by:
David Defenbaugh, Sarah Jang; WS Publishing Group

For more information on this and many other best-selling books visit www.WSPublishingGroup.com.
E-mail: info@WSPublishingGroup.com

ISBN 13: 978-1-934386-99-6

Printed in China

Write a WARNING

on this page to anyone who finds this book.

B.U.S.H.

acro•nym
noun

1: formed from the initial letter
or letters of each of the parts
<I like to mock the president
with this acronym>

puzzle • wordgame • acrostic • composition

Complete this
ACRONYM:

B ....

U ....

S ....

H ....

su•pe•ri•or
adjective

2: of higher rank, quality, or importance
4: excellent of its kind: better
<Democrats are clearly the superior party>

greater • excellent • high-caliber • first-rate • premium

List all the reasons Liberals are SUPERIOR to Conservatives.

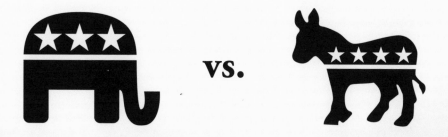

vs.

de•face
verb

1 a: to corrupt the purity
or perfection of
<I will feel better about
politics after I deface
this journal>

abuse • besmirch • dirty • pollute • sully • tarnish

Your face would look
much better like this

 Glue a picture of your most hated Conservative here and DEFACE it. Draw horns, fangs, or a mustache on it.

exile
noun

1: to be deported or forced
from one's country or home
<I would like to exile all
Conservatives to Siberia>

banish • cast out • discard • oust • expulse • sayonara

Make a list of the annoying
Conservative celebrities you wish
would be EXILED to another country.

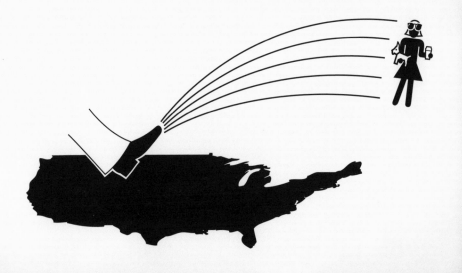

guise
noun

2: a purpose or motive alleged or an
appearance assumed in order to cloak
the real intention or state of affairs
<WMDs were simply the guise for
attacking Iraq>

pretext • falsehood • appearance • disguise

George W. Bush

What is he best known for?

- ☐ Getting pooped on by a bird during a speech

- ☐ Invading Iraq under the guise of finding Weapons of Mass Destruction, when there weren't any

- ☐ Not finding Bin Laden

- ☐ Dodging two shoes thrown at him by an Iraqi journalist, Matrix-style

tag
verb

1: to deface with graffiti
<I would love to tag crazy Michele
Bachmann's precious vehicle>

brand • deface • mark up • sully • desecrate

TAG Michele Bachmann's car.

Tag it with all the names you'd love to call her.

re•form
verb

1: to put or change into an
improved form or condition
<Republicans want reform,
as long as it doesn't change
anything>

change • convert • fashion • revamp • fine tune

Check off the real reasons Republicans don't like the president's HEALTH CARE REFORM bill?

- ❏ They like to discriminate against people based on gender and preexisting conditions

- ❏ They think your policy should get cancelled if you get too sick

- ❏ If you don't like your current health care plan, you should just lose coverage

- ❏ They don't care about helping low-income people afford health care

- ❏ They don't want taxes for the wealthy to increase

chuck
verb

2 a: toss, throw
<I chucked this paper at
my Republican boss' head>

toss • catapult • heave • throw • fling • lob

Crumple this page into a ball and

CHUCK

IT AT A CONSERVATIVE YOU KNOW.

◆ ◆ ◆ Then walk away like it wasn't you. ◆ ◆ ◆

un•fair
adjective

1: marked by injustice
<It is completely unfair
that George W. Bush
ruined our country>

awry • crooked • flawed • faulty • amiss • uncool

Write about the one **UNFAIR** law or bill that passed and how much that pissed you off.

trick•ster
noun

1: a dishonest person who defrauds others
b: a cunning or deceptive character
<That trickster can't fool me with his
political mumbo-jumbo>

charlatan • con artist • imposter • cheat • swindler

Finding Bin Laden is my <u>top</u> priority.

You can't fool me, you TRICKSTER.

....

....

....

....

....

....

....

....

....

If you think former President Bush has told some great lies, then call him out here.

par•a•dise
noun

2: a place or state of bliss,
felicity, or delight
<A Conservative-free world
would be like paradise>

bliss • joy • ecstasy • serenity • peace • happiness

❖ PARADISE ❖

Describe of a world
without Conservatives.

A world without Conservatives would
be .... !
I would probably celebrate by
.... I would
definitely sleep better at night knowing
that .... would
be out of politics forever and I would
never have to see .... 's
annoying face ever again. Imagine how
.... the world would
be without .... rambling
on and on? Why doesn't someone send
all Conservatives to .... ?

con•ser•va•tive
adjective

1: disposed to maintain existing
views, conditions, or institutions
<Conservative spending means
wasting our tax money>

status quo • guarded • stuck in a rut • fearful

THE **CONSERVATIVE** ECONOMIC STIMULUS PACKAGE INCLUDES:

- Building more gas-guzzling Hummers

- Take money from social welfare programs and use it to buy weapons

- Helping Rush Limbaugh buy a sports team

- Bonuses for big-business CEOS

- Donations to keep Fox News running

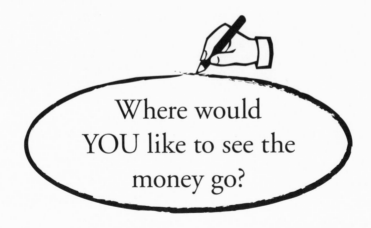

Where would YOU like to see the money go?

res•cue
verb

1: to free from confinement,
danger, or evil
<Someone please rescue me
from Glenn!>

salvage • liberate • free • relieve • get out

RESCUE ME!

What are three things you'd need if you were stranded on a desert island with GLENN BECK for eternity?

 ....

 ....

 ....

#*@%!!!

rogue
adjective

1: being aberrant, dangerous,
or uncontrollable
<The Republican party's
little plan backfired when
Palin went rogue>

wild • undisciplined • uncontained • loose canon

Sarah Palin

What is she best known for?

- Going rogue

- Seeing Russia from her house in Alaska

- Her underage knocked-up daughter

- Completely ruining John McCain's chances

sar•cas•tic
adjective

1: joking or jesting often inappropriately
2: meant to be humorous or funny, not serious
<When I say I don't hate Conservatives,
I'm being sarcastic>

fake • false • guileful • insincere • phony • facetious

Write a **sarcastic** note
to everyone who doesn't vote.

Dear People
Who Don't Vote,

pris•on•ers
noun

1: individuals in captivity for
committing a crime
<Why doesn't Bill O'Reilly
interview some of the Gitmo
prisoners on his show?>

subversive • insurgent • rebel • detainee

Where would you like to send the Gitmo
PRISONERS
after Obama closes that awful place?

- ❑ Republican National Headquarters

- ❑ George Bush's ranch

- ❑ On Sarah Palin's book tour

- ❑ Hunting with Cheney

- ❑ Karl Rove's house for dinner

- ❑ "The O'Reilly Factor"

stream of con•scious•ness
noun

1: the continuous unedited
chronological flow of conscious
experience through the mind
<No one wants to be in my
stream of consciousness>

free association • inner monologue • train of thought

FU STREAM OF CONSCIOUSNESS

Write the first thing that comes to your mind:

Health care reform: ....

....

Taxes: ....

....

War: ....

....

Gay marriage: ....

....

Global Warming: ....

....

Immigration: ....

....

Missile defense system: ....

....

Stem cell research: ....

....

Homeland Security: ....

....

des•pise
verb

1: to look down on with
contempt or aversion
<I despise ultra-Republican
John Kyl>

abhor • disregard • scorn • loathe • dislike

Who is your most
DESPISED
political figure?

Label this voodoo doll as your
most hated political figure.
Tear it at out, hang it on
the wall, and throw
darts at it.

mo•ron
noun

2: a very stupid person
<You Mr. Ex-President,
are a moron>

blockhead • dimwit • idiot • dunce • imbecile

Dear **Moron**,

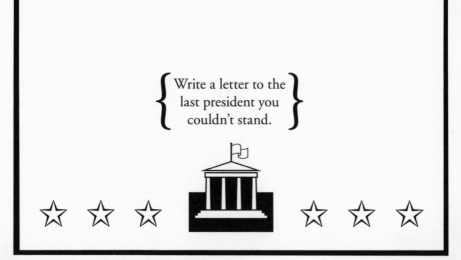

{ Write a letter to the
last president you
couldn't stand. }

in•com•pe•tent
adjective

3 a: lacking the qualities needed for
effective action
b: unable to function properly
<Republicans are incompetent when it
comes to helping anyone but themselves>

bush-league • unskilled • inept • unqualified • unfit

INCOMPETENT
— SPENDING —

Describe what you think the Conservatives
really do with your tax money?

suck
adjective

1: markedly inferior in
quality : lousy, inadequate
<Don't you wish Obama
had yelled "You suck"
back at Joe Wilson?>

crummy • junky • lousy • shoddy • inferior • third rate

YOU SUCK

!!!!!!!!!!!

• • • • • • • • • • •

Remember when Republican Congressman Joe Wilson
yelled out "You lie!" in the middle of Congress?

What would you like to yell back at him
and all his Conservative cohorts?

cel•e•brate
verb

2 a: to honor by refraining from ordinary business
b: to mark by festivities or other deviation from routine
<I plan to celebrate the fact that he was impeached>

party • paint the town red • let loose • rejoice • fiesta

CELEBRATE!

Pretend the Republican who sucks
the most is getting impeached.

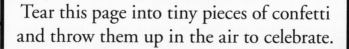

Tear this page into tiny pieces of confetti
and throw them up in the air to celebrate.

un•pop•u•lar
adjective

1: viewed or received unfavorably
<Ha ha, Cheney is even
unpopular with his own party>

abhorred • avoided • creepy • despised • unliked

ᘓ FORMER *ᘔ*
VICE PRESIDENT

Dick Cheney

What is he best known for?

☐ John McCain asking him not to attend the Republican Convention because he was so unpopular

☐ Waterboarding a detainee 183 times

☐ Being chairman and CEO of corrupt Halliburton

☐ Shooting a buddy with buckshot during a hunting trip

be•rate
verb

1: to scold or condemn
vehemently and at length
<I will berate you with
this letter>

badmouth • bash • slam • offend • smear • zing

Berate a Conservative of your choice.

Dear ....,

You suck so much, I want to throw
.... at you.
Listening to you speak makes me want
to ....
When I found out you got elected,
I wanted to ....
A .... would be better
in office than you. Why don't you
move to ....
for .... years?

Sincerely,

....

global warm•ing
noun

1: an increase in the earth's atmospheric
and oceanic temperatures due to pollution
<Ignore global warming and see what
happens, Conservative morons>

In a recent poll, GLOBAL WARMING
was the issue Republicans cared least about.
What are the real reasons Conservatives don't
care about the environment?

❑ They want to drill for oil in Alaska

❑ They hate the tree frogs

❑ They believe global warming is a Liberal hoax

❑ They hate the color green

❑ They have a personal vendetta against Al Gore

❑ The Christian Right believes the Apocalypse
is coming anyway

❑ All of the above

married
noun

1: being in the state of love
and legal matrimony
<Being married stinks:
Why do Conservatives care
if gay people do it too?>

joined • bonded • unioned • wed • esposed

Why don't Republicans want to let gay couples get MARRIED?

 It's not the Christian thing to do

 What's next? People marrying animals?!

 Gay couples will probably vote Democrat

 It might make more gay Republican politicians come out of the closet

im•ple•ment
verb

1: to carry out; accomplish to give
practical effect to and ensure of actual
fulfillment by concrete measures
<I'm surprised the Conservatives
haven't implemented a ban on divorce>

enable • put in place • make possible • enact

If you were a politician, what is the first law you would **implement**?

Write your law here

brain•storm•ing
verb

1: the mulling over of ideas
<I enjoy brainstorming
ways to take down the
Conservative movement>

analyze • conceive • put heads together • concoct

FU Brainstorming Session

stubburn

greedy

uncreative

Vandalize this page with all the
words that describe Conservatives.

double agent
noun

1: a spy pretending to serve
one government while
actually serving another
<I suspect John McCain is
a double agent>

inside man • spy • mole • undercover agent • informer

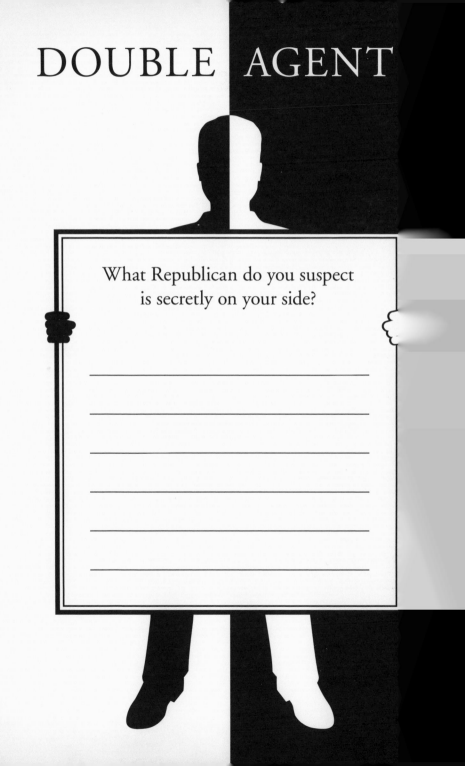

pri•or•i•ty
noun

3: something given attention
before competing alternatives
<Conservatives should try
making real people
their priority>

first concern • precendence • rank • superiority

Who is the Conservatives' top **PRIORITY** when it comes to human stem cell research?

(Protecting the rights of embryonic cells in a Petri dish)

or

(Finding a cure for millions of people with cancer, Parkinson's, Alzheimer's, diabetes, heart disease, and spinal cord injuries)

Circle the group who is most important to Conservatives.

award
noun

2: something that is conferred or
bestowed especially on the basis of merit
<I present you with the award for
the shadiest Conservative ever>

distinction • honor • prize • badge • accolade • ribbon

Give someone this AWARD.

CONGRATULATIONS

_____!

You have won the distinction of
dumbest Conservative on the planet.

_____

_____

_____

_____

_____

_____

_____

_____

#1 Loser

mock•ing
verb

1: treating with contempt or ridicule
<Ann Coulter's mocking of
politicians and war heroes makes
people of both parties hate her>

belittling • deriding • scoffing • ridiculing

Ann Coulter

What is she best known for?

- ❑ Saying, after 9/11, "We should invade their countries, kill their leaders and convert them to Christianity"

- ❑ Closely resembling a shrew

- ❑ Being fired from MSNBC for mocking a disabled Vietnam War veteran on air

- ❑ Calling John Edwards a "faggot"

back off
verb

1: to withdraw from a position
<I told my coworker to back
off with the political rants>

retreat • resign • yield • wither • submit • fend off

Back Off!

Tell Liberals how you feel. Trace your hand on this page with your middle finger raised and decorate it.

spell
noun

1 a: spoken word or set of words
believed to have magic power
<I cast a spell on him; he will
now turn into a pig>

hex • conjuring • magic • mojo • sorcery • wizardry • jinx

CAST A SPELL

on a Conservative who annoys
the crap out of you.

INSTRUCTIONS:

- Pour ½ cup of red wine into a bowl.
- Break a pen and pour the ink into the mixture.
- Add two dashes of garlic salt.
- Drop in a pinch of staples.
- Mix counterclockwise.

Now, check off which effect you want
the spell to have on your foe.

☐ A week of bad luck

☐ Can't find his or her car keys

☐ Grow a tail

☐ Smell like rotten fish

hush
verb

1: calm or quiet
2: to keep from public knowledge
<Liberals won't hush until Don't Ask,
Don't Tell is overturned>

silence • quiet • shush • shut up • suppress

 HUSH …
Don't Ask, Don't Tell!

Don't Ask, Don't Tell is a/n ....

.... policy. The fact that it is

still around is ....

John McCain and other ....

Conservatives think we should keep the status

quo, but Don't Ask, Don't Tell is ....

.... and ....

We should be ....

that brave men and women want to fight in

our military. President Obama is ....

.... for wanting to overturn it.

fan•tasy
noun

1: the power or process of
creating especially unrealistic
or improbable mental images
<In my fantasy, there are no
Republicans in government>

daydream • utopia • fairytale • dream • bubble

★ Fill out your **fantasy** ballot. ★

President: ....

Vice President: ....

Secretary of State: ....

Secretary of the Treasury: ....

Attorney General: ....

Secretary of Defense: ....

Secretary of Homeland Security: ....

Governor of your state: ....

.................................: ....

.................................: ....

.................................: ....

buzz•word
noun

1: an important-sounding usually
technical word or phrase often of little
meaning used chiefly to impress laymen
<I can't make sense of Conservative
buzzwords>

bunk • cliché • mumbo jumbo • lingo • nonsense

BUZZWORD

Abstinence	Privatized health care	Tax cuts	Stay the course	Brainstorm
Personal accounts	Streamline	Status quo	Sanctity of marriage	Drug regulation
Grassroots	Think outside the box	**FREE SPACE**	Compassionate Conservative	Bleeding heart Liberals
Mudslinging	No child left behind	Pro-Life	Visionary	Border security
Supply side economics	Junk science	Axis of Evil	Feed the beast	Synergy

B^{FU}iNGO

Put an X through the box each time you hear annoying Conservative jargon.

va•moose
verb

1: to depart quickly,
to disappear
<I am packed and
ready to vamoose>

run away • bolt • escape • quit • make a break for it

TIME TO VAMOOSE!

I would pack my bags and
move to Switzerland if ...

....

....

....

....

....

....

loos•en up
verb

1: to become less tense
<I need to loosen up
with a stiff drink>

balm • pacify • placate • calm • tranquilize • ease

Loosen the
F#@K UP

Make a list of the ways you can
get your mind off politics.

pin
verb

2: to assign the blame
or responsibility for
<I'd like to pin
the blame on the
Conservatives>

stick • attach • fasten • affix • press

PIN THE TIE ON THE ELEPHANT:

Devious and arrogant GOP mastermind Karl Rove.
Tear out this sheet. Hang it on the wall.

syn•o•nym
noun

1: one of two or more words or
expressions of the same language that
have the same meaning
<Match these synonyms, if you can wade
through the Conservative propaganda>

glossary • lexicon • terminology • vocabulary

❧ FU SYNONYMS ☙

Match these Conservative terms with their real definitions

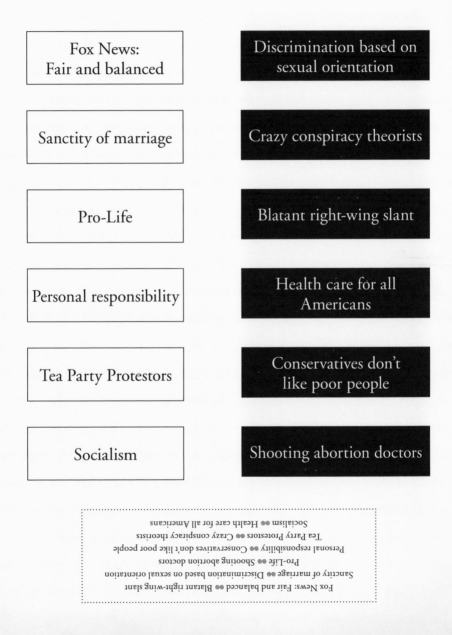

Fox News: Fair and balanced	Discrimination based on sexual orientation
Sanctity of marriage	Crazy conspiracy theorists
Pro-Life	Blatant right-wing slant
Personal responsibility	Health care for all Americans
Tea Party Protestors	Conservatives don't like poor people
Socialism	Shooting abortion doctors

Fox News: Fair and balanced ●● Blatant right-wing slant
Sanctity of marriage ●● Discrimination based on sexual orientation
Pro-Life ●● Shooting abortion doctors
Personal responsibility ●● Conservatives don't like poor people
Tea Party Protestors ●● Crazy conspiracy theorists
Socialism ●● Health care for all Americans

pissed
adjective

1: bitter in spirit: irritated
<Caution: Pissed off
Liberal behind the wheel>

bitter • dismal • crestfallen • annoyed • dejected

Pissed off?

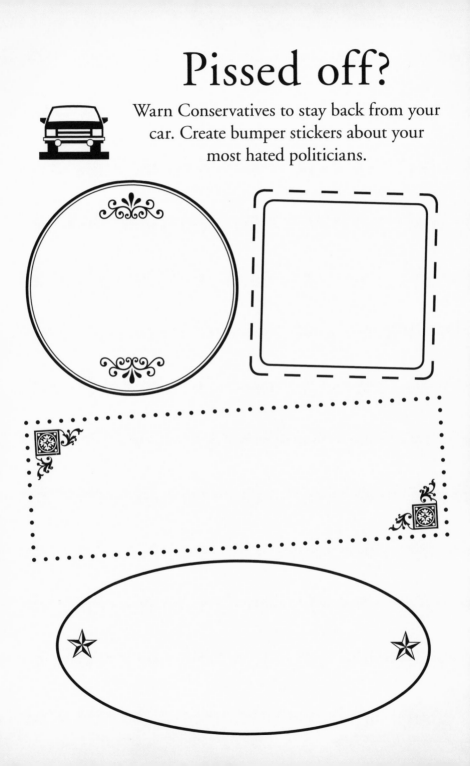

Warn Conservatives to stay back from your car. Create bumper stickers about your most hated politicians.

false
adjective

1: the nature of being untrue
<Conservatives love to spread
false accusations about the
ACORN organization>

made up • untrue • imaginary • wrong • misleading

ACORN

TRUE OR FALSE

T or **F**

☐ ☐ Conservatives believe that Acorn committed voter fraud to help Obama win the election

☐ ☐ Shady "journalists" want to imply corruption because Conservatives don't like social welfare programs

☐ ☐ Help families in low-income areas avoid foreclosure

☐ ☐ Education and assistance for families in poverty

☐ ☐ Conservatives cut funding to a helpful organization because of five bad apples

haz•ard
noun

1: a source of danger
<Conservatives are a
hazard to my health>

imperilment • jeopardy • peril • risk • thin ice

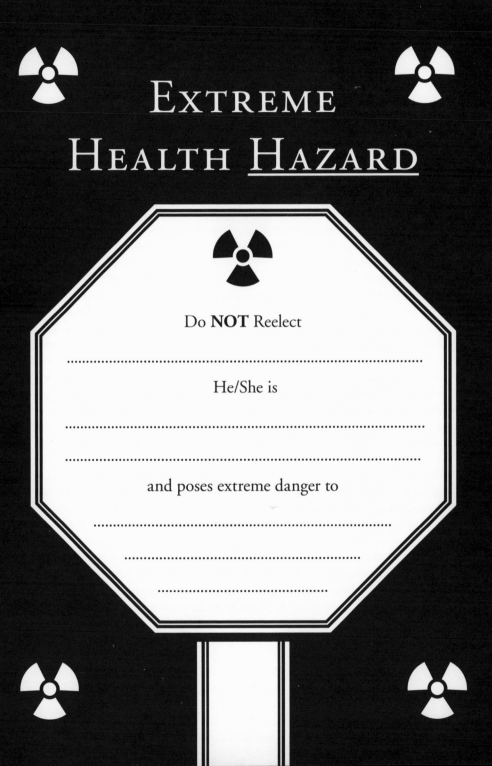

EXTREME HEALTH HAZARD

Do **NOT** Reelect

....

He/She is

....

....

and poses extreme danger to

....

....

....

crush
noun

3 a: an intense and usually
passing infatuation
b: the object of infatuation
<None of my Liberal friends
can know of my crush>

flame • love affair • passion • puppy love • enamor

non•sen•si•cal
adjective

1 a: words or language having
no meaning or conveying no
intelligible ideas
<Bush was the king of saying
totally nonsensical things>

foolish • ridiculous • senseless • stupid • inane

Name that quote! Who said each of these NONSENSICAL quotes?

"I hear there's rumors on the Internets that we're going to have a draft."

....
(name that person)

"The most important thing is for us to find Osama bin Laden. It is our number one priority and we will not rest until we find him."

....
(name that person)

"Those weapons of mass destruction have got to be somewhere!"

....
(name that person)

"Our enemies are innovative and resourceful, and so are we. They never stop thinking about new ways to harm our country and our people, and neither do we."

....
(name that person)

po•lit•i•cal
adjective

1: the conduct of someone
with questionable and
tactical motives
<Michele Bachmann's
actions are purely political>

cunning • crafty • tactical • calculated • strategic

Political Word Search

t	r	b	i	r	i	l	t	i	b	f	v	a
n	d	b	e	t	a	b	e	d	v	a	d	t
e	v	i	t	a	v	r	e	s	n	o	c	u
m	i	l	y	n	o	f	c	l	n	n	c	n
n	h	l	i	b	e	r	a	l	y	d	l	n
o	l	c	s	n	m	d	m	c	c	a	i	n
r	s	e	s	s	n	r	i	c	n	b	n	y
i	p	e	a	a	e	l	s	s	t	v	t	m
v	u	h	c	r	o	r	p	e	e	i	o	o
n	n	s	k	p	s	s	g	t	n	r	n	n
e	d	u	c	a	t	i	o	n	s	a	p	o
a	i	b	e	y	a	m	a	b	o	q	t	c
e	t	a	b	e	d	h	n	n	i	c	a	e

Liberal	Senate	Debate	Iraq
Conservative	Congress	Environment	Israel
Policy	Pundit	Clinton	Hannity
Bill	Defense	Obama	Beck
President	Economy	McCain	Scandal
Veto	Education	Bush	Debate

ha•rass•ment
noun

1: uninvited and unwelcome verbal
or physical behavior by a person in
authority toward a subordinate
<It's about time someone called
Bill O'Reilly out for harassment>

badgering • nuisance • bashing • tormenting

Bill O'Reilly

What is he best known for?

☐ His insistence that organized secular progressives are trying to ruin Christmas, and that the term "Happy Holidays" is anti-Christian

☐ His ongoing feud with Keith Olbermann, who crowned him "Worst Person in the World"

☐ Saying, "I just wish Katrina had only hit the United Nations building, nothing else, just flooded them out. And I wouldn't have rescued them."

☐ The nickname Falafel Man from his sexual harassment lawsuit

scrib•ble
verb

1: to write hastily or carelessly without regard
to legibility or form
2: to cover with careless or worthless writings
or drawings
<When I scribble in this journal, I feel better>

doodle • jot • scratch • scrawl • squiggle

Scribble

on this page as hard
as you can.

Take out your frustration with politics here.

blunt
adjective

3 a: abrupt in speech or manner
b: being straight to the point
<Let me be blunt: You all suck>

direct • unsubtle • outspoken • honest • candid

Draft the email you wish you could send to all your irrational Conservative friends.

Subject: The **Blunt** Truth

To: All my Conservative friends

Cc: Republican Party

Send

night•mare
noun

3: an experience, situation, or object
having monstrous character or
producing a feeling of anxiety or terror
<Sarah Palin becoming president
would be a complete nightmare>

horror • frightening • terror • scare • hallucination

⚘ Political ⚘ NIGHTMARE.

Who would you rather see run for office in 2012 than Sarah Palin?

- ☐ A goat
- ☐ Vladimir Putin
- ☐ Newt Gingrich
- ☐ Meghan McCain
- ☐ Other: ....

cir•cum•vent
verb

2: to manage to get around
especially by ingenuity or stratagem
<This maze reminds me of how
Republicans always circumvent
tough questions>

skirt • evade • sidestep • bypass • dodge • avoid

Make your way through this maze to the White House, but be sure to ⇥ CIRCUMVENT ⇤ all the Conservative crap.

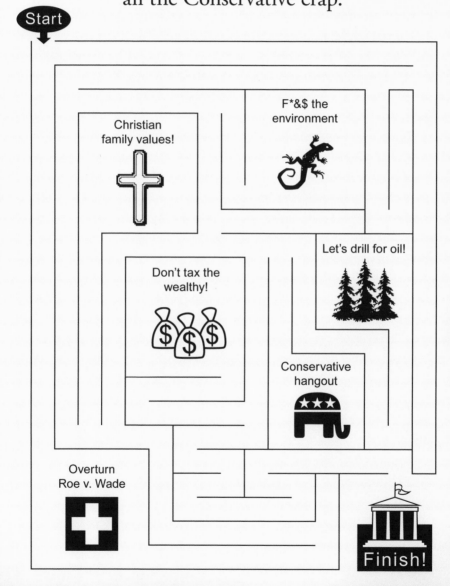

picket
verb

1: to protest against for a cause
<I would like to picket
against sending more troops
to Afghanistan with no exit
strategy>

boycott • demonstrate • strike • hit the bricks • protest

FU PICKET SIGN

Create a **picket** sign to protest the most annoying Conservative issue.

in•fu•ri•at•ing
adjective

1: to have been made furious
<Conservative politics are
completely infuriating>

aggravating • enraging • frustrating • blood-boiling

Conservative Health Care Reform:

What is the most **infuriating** part?

❑ Senator John Kyl saying health insurance providers should not have to cover maternity care — because he doesn't need it

❑ "President Obama wants to kill old people!"

❑ Insurers would still be able to block coverage for people with preexisting conditions

❑ The Stupak Amendment, which would expand a ban on government funding for abortion coverage

❑ Conservative bill wouldn't even extend coverage to 52 million uninsured Americans

cheap shot
noun

2: a critical statement that
takes unfair advantage of a
known weakness of the target
<I'd like to take a cheap
shot at Newt Gingrich>

backbite • knock • hit • slander • snub

FU
CHEAP SHOT

Make a list of your most hated Conservative
politician's faults and screw ups.

....

....

....

....

....

....

....

....

....

....

....

....

smear
verb

1: to vilify especially by secretly
and maliciously spreading grave
charges and imputations
<Glenn Beck's job is essentially
one giant smear campaign>

sully • tarnish • besmirch • dirty • vilify

FOX NEWS STOOGE

Glenn Beck

What is he best known for?

- ☐ Leading the Conservative smear campaign against Van Jones, leading to his resignation

- ☐ Promoting the undercover videos of ACORN employees being set up, which forced to the government to stop funding the organization

- ☐ Being a former drug addict and alcoholic with only a high school education

- ☐ Saying Barack Obama is a racist and hates white people, causing 80 advertisers to pull their ads from his program

hy•poc•ri•sy
noun

1: a feigning to be what one is not or to
believe what one does not; especially : the
false assumption of an appearance of virtue
<Conservative hypocrisy makes me laugh>

falsity • fraud • insincerity • lies • duplicity

☞ Favorite example of Conservative HYPOCRISY?

 Senator Larry Craig, a staunch anti-gay activist, soliciting sex from a male undercover cop in an airport bathroom

 Attorney General Eliot Spitzer spending $80,000 on call girls despite claiming to fight prostitution and organized crime

 Congressman Mark Foley making sexual advances at teenage male pages while leading a national campaign against child pornography

 Abstinence supporter Sarah Palin's 16-year-old daughter getting pregnant

Do as we say, not as we do.

Ding! Ding!

blood•bath
noun

2: a notably fierce, violent, or
destructive contest or struggle
<A fight between Ann Coulter
and President Obama would
be a bloodbath>

massacre • carnage • slaughter • annihilation • fight

Let the **Bloodbath** Begin!

Write who you would like to see go head-to-head in a boxing match.

In the Liberal corner we have …

In the Conservative corner we have …

mot•to
noun

1: a sentence, phrase, or word inscribed
on something as appropriate to or
indicative of its character or use
<My campaign motto would be "FU
Conservatives">

slogan • aphorism • byword • epigram • maxim • proverb

CAMPAIGN MOTTO

If you were running for president,
what would your slogan be?

hunt•ing
verb

1: the pursuit of game, for shooting
<Conservatives don't care about the
environment, but they sure love hunting>

track • shoot • pursue • stalk • kill • capture

Conservative **hunting** trip.
It's open season for:

Alaskan moose

Illegal immigrants

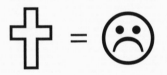

Atheists

Endangered Northern
Spotted Owls

Dick Cheney's
buddies

Circle the group that Conservatives
⤜⬥ would love to hunt. ⬥⤛

los•er
noun

1: a person or thing that loses especially consistently
2: a person who is incompetent or unable to succeed; something doomed to fail or disappoint
<These crazy right-wing Republicans are losers>

dud • failure • deadbeat • flop • flunkee • waste of space

BIGGEST LOSER

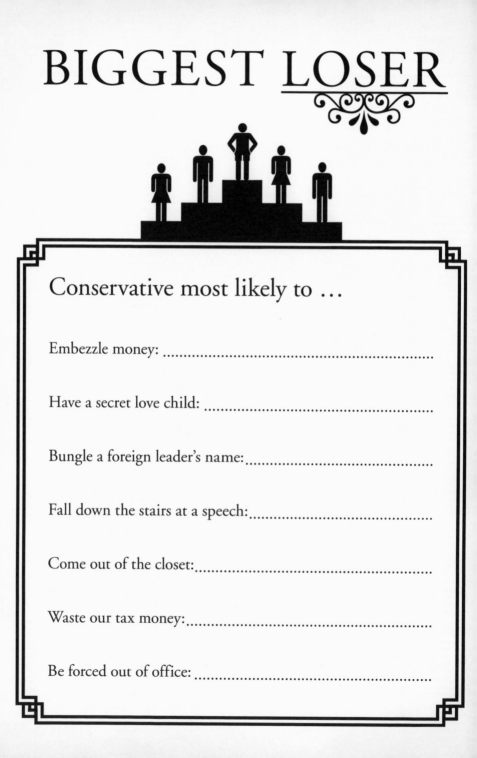

Conservative most likely to …

Embezzle money: ....

Have a secret love child: ....

Bungle a foreign leader's name: ....

Fall down the stairs at a speech: ....

Come out of the closet: ....

Waste our tax money: ....

Be forced out of office: ....

un•qual•i•fied
adjective

1: not having requisite
qualifications
<Sarah Palin was about as
unqualified as you could get
— way to go McCain>

permissive • passive • socialist • pushover

2008 REPUBLICAN CANDIDATE FOR PRESIDENT

John McCain

What is he best known for?

○ Being the oldest person ever to run for president

○ Admitting he doesn't email and is just learning to use the Internet

○ Bluffing that he would suspend his campaign to "work on a bailout plan" in hopes of avoiding a debate with Barack Obama

○ Choosing unqualified Sarah Palin as his vice presidential running mate

guilty
adjective

1: responsible for a grave
breach of conduct
<The Republican party is
guilty of a lot of shadiness>

blameworthy • liable • at fault • shady

GUILTY BY
ASSOCIATION

List the corrupt people you think the
Republican party should not fraternize with:

rather
adverb

1: more readily or willingly
<I would rather eat dog food
than become a Republican>

considerably • noticeably • quite • much

Would you **rather** …

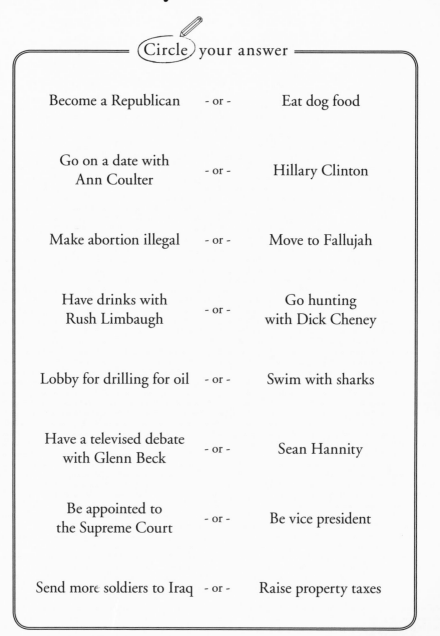

Circle your answer

Become a Republican	- or -	Eat dog food
Go on a date with Ann Coulter	- or -	Hillary Clinton
Make abortion illegal	- or -	Move to Fallujah
Have drinks with Rush Limbaugh	- or -	Go hunting with Dick Cheney
Lobby for drilling for oil	- or -	Swim with sharks
Have a televised debate with Glenn Beck	- or -	Sean Hannity
Be appointed to the Supreme Court	- or -	Be vice president
Send more soldiers to Iraq	- or -	Raise property taxes

cre•a•tive
adjective

1: the ability to be
artistic; imaginative
<This journal lets
me be creative while
venting about politics>

clever • inspired • productive • imaginative • visionary

FU Creative
Writing Assignment

Complete this poem.
There once was a
Conservative from Nantucket ...

....
....
....
....
....
....
....
....
....

bud•dy-bud•dy
adjective

1: familiarly friendly
<I wouldn't mind being
buddy-buddy with
Arnold Schwarzenegger >

chummy • affectionate • close • comfortable • intimate

cra•zy
adjective

2: mad, insane
<Rush Limbaugh is
obviously completely crazy>

batty • insane • nuts • losing it • ranting

What is the CRAZIEST thing you've heard **Rush Limbaugh** say?

joke
noun

1: a brief oral narrative with a climactic humorous twist
b: the humorous or ridiculous element in something
<I like making a joke at a Conservative's expense>

prank • farce • humor • shenanigan • wisecrack

Tell your favorite
Conservative-bashing joke.

Ha
ha
ha

Q: What's the difference between the Vietnam War and the Iraq War?

A: George W. Bush had a plan to get out of the Vietnam War.

Q: ....

....

....

A: ....

....

....

shut up
verb

1: to cause a person to stop talking
<I wish I could tell my Conservative
friends to shut up>

clam up • hush • quiet down • zip it • settle

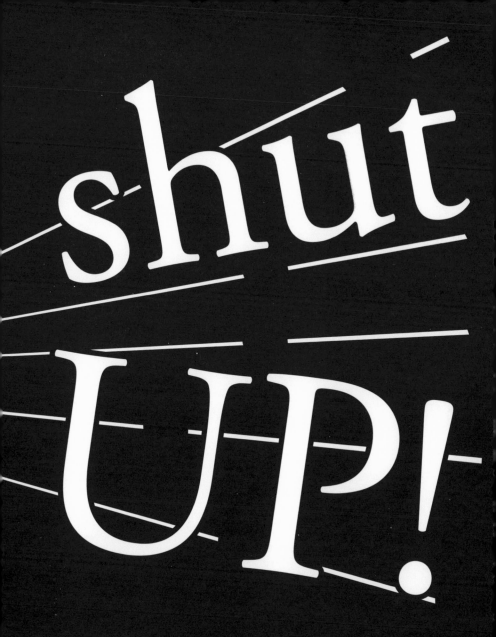

shut
UP!

Point this page at your Conservative friends
the next time they are complaining to you.

nat•u•ral•iz•ing
verb

1: to admit to citizenship
<GOP: Why the sudden interest in
naturalizing immigrants, hmmm?>

acclimate • confirm • adapt • include • award

What is the real reason Conservatives are reconsidering <u>NATURALIZING</u> illegal immigrants?

- ❏ They care about the plight of hardworking immigrant families living in America

- ❏ Deporting everyone sounds like a hassle

- ❏ They don't want to lose their nannies and housekeepers

- ❏ They're scared the Minutemen militia are getting too out of control

- ❏ They know they need Latino votes for to the 2012 election

scan•dal
noun

3: a circumstance or action that offends
propriety or established moral conceptions
or disgraces those associated with it
<Newt Gingrich is no stranger to scandal>

embarrassment • dirty laundry • skeleton in the closet

Newt Gingrich

What is he best known for?

- ☐ Marrying his former teacher at age 19
- ☐ Saying that "waterboarding is not torture"
- ☐ Idolizing Ronald Reagan
- ☐ Having his own extramarital affair while leading the case against Bill Clinton during the Monica Lewinsky scandal

pro•test•er
noun

1: to make a statement or
gesture in objection to
<I wish these protesters
would give it up>

heckler • militant • radical • rebel • troublemaker

Tea Party PROTESTERS

— Even the GOP is embarrassed of them!
Write what you think of them.

im•pale
verb

2: to pierce with something pointed
<I would like to impale the real
Michele Bachmann with a sword>

lance • prick • skewer • spike • stick • gouge

mis•rep•re•sen•ta•tion
noun

1: to give a false or misleading representation of,
usually with an intent to deceive or be unfair
<People who chain themselves to trees are a
misrepresentation of Liberals>

falsehood • distortion • false light • slant • lie

FU Liberal Misrepresentation

Dispel one of the most popular misconceptions about Liberals.

....

....

....

....

....

....

....

....

....

....

....

blind

adjective

1: unable or unwilling to discern or judge
2: having no regard to rational discrimination, guidance, or restriction
<The Birthers just turn a blind eye on reality>

avoiding reality • thoughtless • in the dark

List the words you would use to describe the "Birthers" who STILL believe President Obama wasn't born in the U.S.

Conspiracy theorists

BLIND

Sore losers

mas•cot
noun

1: a person, animal, or thing adopted
by a group as a symbolic figure
<The elephant is a perfect mascot,
because Republicans are fat and slow>

representation • symbol • charm • object

Introducing the new Republican party
☆ ★ ☆ MASCOT ☆ ★ ☆

Draw the animal that should *really*
represent the Republican party

im•pres•sion
noun

1: an imitation or
representation of someone
<My impression isn't as
crazy as the real Bush>

imitation • parody • representation • pretending